THAT'S GROSS!

GROSS THINGS ABOUT YOUR PETS

By Julie Marzolf

 Gareth Stevens
Publishing

Please visit our website, www.garethstevens.com. For a free color catalog of all our high-quality books, call toll free 1-800-542-2595 or fax 1-877-542-2596.

Library of Congress Cataloging-in-Publication Data

Marzolf, Julie Schwab.
 Gross things about your pets / Julie Marzolf.
     p. cm. — (That's gross!)
 Includes bibliographical references and index.
ISBN 978-1-4339-7120-4 (pbk.)
ISBN 978-1-4339-7121-1 (6-pack)
ISBN 978-1-4339-7119-8 (library binding)
1. Pets—Miscellanea—Juvenile literature. 2. Curiosities and wonders—Juvenile literature. I. Title.
 SF416.2.M28 2013
 636.088'7—dc23

2012007447

First Edition

Published in 2013 by
Gareth Stevens Publishing
111 East 14th Street, Suite 349
New York, NY 10003

Designer: Benjamin Gardner
Editor: Therese Shea

Photo credits: Cover, p. 1 (puppies) Wallenrock/Shutterstock.com; Cover, p. 1 (insect) Science Photo Library/E. GRAY/SPL/Getty Images; p. 5 Vitelle/Shutterstock.com; p. 7 Dmitry Kalinovsky/Shutterstock.com; p. 9 © iStockphoto.com/Marian Pentek; p. 11 © iStockphoto.com/4loops; p. 13 (fish tank) MattJones/Shutterstock.com; p. 13 (algae) © iStockphoto.com/spxChrome; p. 15 Perig/Shutterstock.com; p. 17 Sompoch Tangthai/Shutterstock.com; p. 19 Michelle Lam/Flickr Open/Getty Images; p. 20 Jane Burton/Dorling Kindersley/Getty Images; p. 21 (cat) Tony Campbell/Shutterstock.com; p. 21 (gerbil) Eric Isselée/Shutterstock.com.

Printed in the United States of America

CPSIA compliance information: Batch #CS12GS: For further information contact Gareth Stevens, New York, New York at 1-800-542-2595.

CONTENTS

Words in the glossary appear in **bold** type the first time they are used in the text.

OUR CUTE, GROSS PETS

Pets can be like people in many ways. Dogs like to take walks, want to be loved, and enjoy spending time with their families. Cats like lazy days on the couch, hate taking baths, and love to play.

Pets, like you and me, have good habits and some gross ones, too. This book will tell you about some of the gross things that our pets do. Some things are good for our pets, and some aren't. Pet owners should learn about their pets to keep them healthy and safe.

Gross or Cool?

Dogs and cats sweat through their paws!

Ask an adult to call a **veterinarian**, or vet, if you think your pet is sick.

5

DOGS THAT SCOOT

Have you ever seen a dog drag its bottom along the floor? You might laugh when you see this. However, when a dog drags its behind, it may mean the **sacs** under its tail hurt. These sacs hold an oily **fluid** that dogs use to "mark their territory." The sacs should drain as the dog poops. The smell tells other dogs what dog was there.

However, if the sacs are plugged or **infected**, they feel uncomfortable to the dog. So, a dog drags its behind, like scratching an itch.

There are other reasons a dog might "scoot" across the floor, such as tangled hair. Whatever the dog's reason for scooting, the action tells us that something is wrong.

9

GOOD GROOMING, GROSS HAIRBALLS

Most cats hate water. A cat cleans, or grooms, itself with its tongue. Cat tongues are rough and help get rid of dirt, loose hair, dead skin, and even fleas. Normally these things mix with food and water in a cat's stomach. They leave its body with other waste.

Sometimes hairballs form in a cat's stomach. The cat may cough as it tries to throw up the hair. You can cut down on hairballs by brushing your cat. However, some cats need **medicine** to help with hairballs.

Gross or Cool?

Kittens don't throw up hairballs as often as older cats. This is because they aren't good groomers yet!

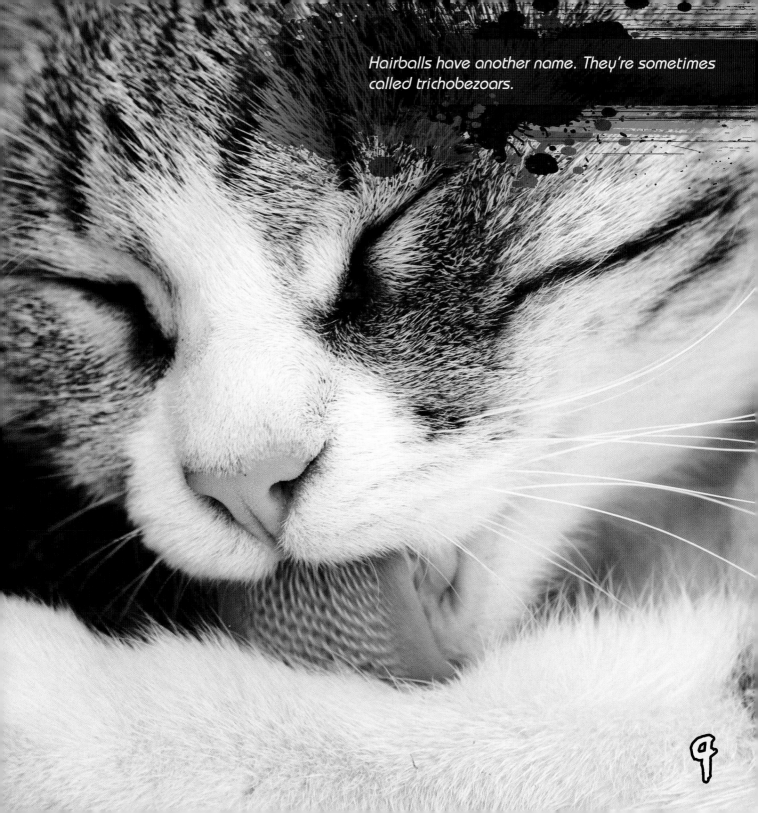

Hairballs have another name. They're sometimes called trichobezoars.

9

BUNNY HAIRBALLS?

Like cats, rabbits use their tongue to groom themselves. So bunnies can get hairballs, too! However, rabbits cannot cough or throw up hairballs like cats do. They have to pass hairballs with their waste. If they don't, they get a condition called gastric stasis.

Gastric stasis means that hair collects in the stomach and stops the movement of food through the **digestive system**. This problem can be deadly. It's important for rabbits to eat the right food so they don't get gastric stasis.

Gastric stasis is deadly because the rabbit stops eating and drinking.

11

CLEAN TANK, HAPPY FISH

Fish that live in tanks breathe in the same water they put their waste into. Gross! Fish waste contains a colorless **chemical** called ammonia. When ammonia builds up in the water, it makes it hard for fish to breathe. This can be deadly.

Filters and clean water in tanks cut down on the amount of ammonia. Some fish owners even grow helpful **bacteria** in their tanks. These bacteria eat ammonia and give off less-harmful chemicals.

Gross or Cool?

High amounts of ammonia can cause fish to make snot, or mucus, that blocks their **gills.**

Keeping your fish tank clean is important for your fishes' health. There are special tools to test the level of ammonia in water.

dirty fish tank

MY DOG ATE WHAT?

Dogs, like people, like to eat lots of different things. However, dogs, especially puppies, sometimes eat poop! They may eat their own waste or that of another animal. The act of an animal eating waste is called coprophagia. Vets don't really know why dogs do this.

If you want your dog to stop this habit, keep your yard clean of waste. Make sure you watch your dog in the yard. If it eats its own waste, ask an adult to call the vet to find out what to do.

Gross or Cool?

Some dog owners put hot sauce on a dog's waste to stop them from eating it. However, some dogs like hot sauce!

Dogs that eat animal waste may be trying to get **nutrients** they aren't getting in their food.

Believe it or not, eating poop is good for rabbits—as long as they eat the right kind. That's still gross! Rabbits produce two kinds of droppings. One is hard, and the other is soft. The soft kind is eaten right away. It still contains some nutrients rabbits need.

Moving the waste through the digestive system a second time helps the rabbit get the most out of its food. Hamsters and guinea pigs eat their own droppings for the same reason.

Rabbits should only eat certain kinds of food, such as vegetables and special rabbit food.

17

CAT JUICE?

Indoor and outdoor cats often like to eat grass. Eating grass may not sound yummy, but it's not harmful to cats. In fact, it may help a cat's health! Cats get folic acid from chewing on the grass and drinking its "juice." Folic acid is a valuable nutrient.

Once cats eat grass, it may help them with hairballs, too. Grass helps cats pass hairballs through their digestive system. The grass might also help them throw up hairballs.

Some kinds of grass and plants aren't healthy for cats to eat. Pet owners should make sure their houseplants aren't poisonous.

19

HAMSTER HOARDERS

The name "hamster" comes from the German word *hamstern*, which means "to hoard." Hoarding is the act of collecting and storing things for the future. And that's just what hamsters do with their food!

Hamsters chew their food and stick it into their cheeks. The food is stored in their cheeks for eating later. Gross! Luckily, their cheeks have special pouches that can hold quite a bit of food. A hamster's mouth is also dry, which helps keep the chewed food from breaking down.

Gross or Cool?

Hamsters' teeth never stop growing. They need to wear them down by chewing on hard things.

Animal Health Cause and Effect

Cause	Effect
Cats swallow their hair while grooming themselves with their tongue.	Cats throw up hairballs.
Some pet owners don't clean their fish tanks.	The ammonia from fish waste in the tanks makes their fish sick.
Rabbits don't get all the nutrients they need from eating.	Rabbits eat their waste to get more nutrients.
Hamsters like to save food for later.	Hamsters save food in their cheek pouches.

GLOSSARY

bacteria: tiny, single-celled organisms. Many kinds are helpful. Some can cause illnesses.

chemical: matter that can be mixed with other matter to cause changes

digestive system: the body system that breaks down food into usable nutrients

filter: a tool through which a gas or liquid is passed to remove matter

fluid: liquid

gill: a body part that fish and other water animals use to breathe

infected: filled with bacteria or other matter that can cause illness

medicine: a drug used to treat an illness

nutrient: something a living thing needs to grow and stay alive

sac: a small pouch inside an animal that often contains a fluid

veterinarian: an animal doctor

22

FOR MORE INFORMATION

Books

Clarke, Ginjer L. *Gross Out! Animals That Do Disgusting Things*. New York, NY: Grosset & Dunlap, 2006.

Green, Gail. *The Kids' Guide to Projects for Your Pet*. Mankato, MN: Capstone Press, 2012.

Rau, Dana Meachen. *Top 10 Fish for Kids*. Berkeley Heights, NJ: Enslow Elementary, 2009.

Websites

ASPCA—Kids
www.aspca.org/aspcakids/
This site has facts, videos, and even games about all kinds of pets.

Pets: Taking Care of Your Pet
pbskids.org/itsmylife/family/pets/article7.html
Learn how to keep your pets safe and healthy.

INDEX